MW00632512

OVERCOME ANXIETY IN RELATIONSHIP

How to Manage Irrational Behaviors, Panic Attacks, Jealousy, Anxiety in Relationship, Codependence, Low Self-Esteem and Prevent Bad Thoughts. How Anxiety Ruins Relationships

Scarlett Williams

Text Copyright©

Legal & Disclaimer

The information contained in this book and its contents is not designed to replace or take the place of any form of medical or professional advice; and is not meant to replace the need for independent medical, financial, legal or other professional advice or services, as may be required. The content and information in this book has been provided for educational and entertainment purposes only.

The content and information contained in this book has been compiled from sources deemed reliable, and it is accurate to the best of the Author's knowledge, information and belief. However, the Author cannot guarantee its accuracy and validity and cannot be held liable for any errors and/or omissions. Further, changes are periodically made to this book as and when needed. Where appropriate and/or necessary, you must consult a professional (including but not limited to your doctor, attorney, financial advisor or such other professional advisor) before using any of the suggested remedies, techniques, or information in this book.

Upon using the contents and information contained in this book, you agree to hold harmless the Author from and against any damages, costs, and expenses, including any legal fees potentially resulting from the application of any of the information provided by this book. This disclaimer applies to any loss, damages or injury caused by the use and application, whether directly or indirectly, of any advice or information presented, whether for breach of contract, tort, negligence, personal injury, criminal intent, or under any other cause of action.

You agree to accept all risks of using the information presented inside this book.

You agree that by continuing to read this book, where appropriate and/or necessary, you shall consult a professional (including but not limited to your doctor, attorney, or financial advisor or such needed) before using any of the suggested remedies, techniques, or information in this book.

Table of Contents

Introduction

Are you constantly anxious in your relationships, worrying that your partner does not love you enough and will leave you? Have you been told you are too sensitive, too clingy, too demanding? Do you feel blocked, suffer from insomnia, nausea, or experience an irregular heartbeat?

These are classic signs of anxiety and stress, and many people get trapped in relationships that stop them from achieving the life and the love they deserve, going around in circles and never resolving any of their problems. You begin to feel as if you are doomed to loneliness and a loveless life, but the good news is that you can rewire your brain to feel happiness in a relationship and stop feeling like you are walking on egg-shells all the time. You can stop being afraid. You can enjoy your relationship.

The author of this has helped thousands of individuals and couples alike to understand their relationship strategies, based on neuroscience. Also, to give them simple but effective advice based on neuroplasticity and behavioral exercises to promote healing from past relationships and to build healthy, exciting, and satisfying relationships.

You will be able to look at yourself objectively, understand how your childhood, your past relationships, and your brain influences your choices and behaviors. You will learn how to tame your thought processes to become clearer, more objective, and able to sustain wonderfully satisfying relationships with people and able to build a strong, lasting bond with a romantic partner.

It will open up your understanding of what jealousy is and why you may be experiencing this feeling. You will understand why jealousy is not considered abnormal and why underlying factors can materialize into jealous feelings. You will learn practical, real-life examples to effectively gain control and eventually overcome your jealousy while keeping your relationship intact. You will also learn to battle insecurities and low confidence so you can feel great and secure about yourself and your relationship again. So why wait?

I have personally battled with jealousy silently for many years. I continued to think I was in control until my jealousy started to get the best of me, and I decided to seek help. I realized I had been mistaken for a long time thinking my partner was the cause of my jealous feelings. I did not know I was the one with the problem. It has been a long journey to recovery, but I can finally say I kicked the green-eyed monster out of my life.

You will emerge a stronger, more confident person from this experience, one that can instantly recognize a good relationship from a bad one and that is capable of cultivating the lasting love you crave.

Dive in right now to start you on your journey to long-lasting love and healthy relating and leave the misery and stress and anxiety behind forever!

Chapter 1: Understanding Your Anxiety in Love

A nxiety can impact your relationships negatively, especially if you spend a great deal of time worrying and thinking about everything that could go wrong or has already gone wrong with the relationship. Here are some questions that may run through your mind when you are too anxious in a relationship:

What if they don't love me as much as I love them?

What if they're lying to me?

What if they're cheating on me?

What if I'm not good enough in the future for them?

What if they find someone else more attractive?

What if their family doesn't love me?

What if they die?

What if my anxiety ruins our relationship? (Anxiety about anxiety)

What if we break up?

What if they bail out on me?

It is normal to have some of these thoughts, especially in a new relationship. However, when thoughts like these come to your mind frequently, it might be a sign of anxiety issues or an anxiety disorder. The intensity with which you constantly ruminate over the questions listed above and other questions that are similar determine how far gone you are into an anxiety problem. It will also determine how insecure you are in your relationship.

These anxious thoughts are manifested in diverse physical ways and present as symptoms such as shortness of breath, insomnia, and anxiety or panic attacks. You may discover that whenever you think this way, you trigger a panic attack in which your heart may begin to beat fast, a hard lump forms in your chest, and you begin to shake all over your body. These are the physiological signs that you are suffering from an anxiety disorder.

Some symptoms of intense anxiety disorder can include:

· A feeling of restlessness

· Tensed muscles

· Difficulty concentrating or remembering

· Procrastinating or having trouble making decisions

· Worry that leads to repeatedly asking for reassurance

· Inability to get enough sleep and rest

Inasmuch as relationships are very beautiful and pleasurable, they can also breed anxious thoughts and feelings. These thoughts can arise at any stage of the relationship. If you aren't in a relationship yet, the thought of meeting the right person and being in a relationship can already generate anxiety for you, which you must deal with.

Insecurity is an inner feeling of not being enough or feeling threatened in some way. We've all felt it at one time or the other. It's quite normal to have feelings of self-doubt once in a while, but chronic insecurity can ruin your success in life and destroy your romantic relationships.

Severe insecurity steals your peace and prevents you from being able to engage with your partner in a relaxed and authentic way. The resultant actions arising from insecurity may include jealousy, false accusations, snooping, lack of trust, and seeking reassurance and validation. These attributes are not conducive to a healthy relationship and can push your partner away.

Most people believe that insecurity stems from the actions or inaction of their partners. The reality is that most insecurity comes from within you. You build insecurity when you negatively compare yourself to other people and judge yourself harshly with your inner critical voice. A lot of the insecurities in your relationship are based on irrational thoughts and fears that you are not good enough and that you are not capable of making someone else happy. But these aren't true!

When you start to notice that uneasy feeling of being insecure, one thing you can do is to begin taking stock of your value. Insecurity makes you focus on something you feel is lacking within you. In most balanced relationships, each partner brings different strengths and qualities that complement each other. In order to conquer your insecurity, take stock of the value you offer to your partner. Personality and a great character are important qualities to the overall health of a relationship.

Building your self-esteem is also crucial to surmounting any insecurity you face in your relationship. It is important that you feel good about who you are on the inside in order to not constantly seek validation from someone else. You are complete within yourself and you must let your independence and self-worth shine brightly through your deeds and actions. When your well-being depends on someone else, you give them the key to your joy, and you empower them. This may be quite unhealthy for your partner to bear and certainly does not work well for a relationship. One way to build your self-confidence is to silence your inner critic and focus your mind and attention on positive qualities. Look in the mirror and speak positive affirmations to yourself - looking yourself in the eye when you do this makes a greater impact than simply telling yourself in your head that you're worthy of love.

You should also be able to maintain your sense of self-identity and be able to cater to your personal well-being. If before the relationship you were doing a great job of tending to your physical, mental, and emotional needs, this should not stop now just because you are in a relationship. You should maintain your independence and not allow yourself to turn into someone who is needy or attached. Being an independent person who has a life and identity outside of the relationship also makes you a more interesting and attractive partner. Your life must continue to move forward and make considerable progress when you are in a relationship. Being in a relationship is not the final phase of your life, and you should continue to be driven and achieve more goals, which can further endear you to your partner.

Some ways to maintain your independence include cultivating and nurturing great friendships, making time for your own friends, interests, and hobbies, maintaining financial independence, constantly improving yourself, and setting high standards for your dreams.

Understanding Why You Feel Anxious, Insecure and Attached in Relationships

Worry, stress, and anxiety about your relationships can leave you feeling lonely and dejected. You may unknowingly create a distance between yourself and your loved one. Another grave consequence of anxiety is its ability to make us give up on love completely. That is rather devastating, because love is a very beautiful thing. It is important to really understand what makes you so anxious in a relationship and why you feel so insecure and attached. I will take you through some of the reasons in subsequent paragraphs.

Falling in love puts a demand on you in countless ways - more ways than you can imagine. The more you cherish a person, the more you stand to lose. How ironic is that? This intense feeling of love and the powerful emotions that come with it consciously and unconsciously create the fear of being hurt and the fear of the unknown in you.

Oddly enough, this fear comes as a result of being treated exactly how you want to be treated in your relationship. When you begin to

16

experience love as it should be, or when you are treated in tender and caring way, which is unfamiliar to you, anxiety might set in.

More often than not, it is not only the events that occur between you and your partner that lead to anxiety. It is the things you tell yourself and feed your mind with regarding those events that ultimately lead to anxiety. Your biggest critic, which is also the "mean coach" you have in your head, can criticize you and feed you with bad advice which will ultimately fuel your fear of intimacy. It is this mean critic that suggests to you that:

"You are not smart, he/she would soon get bored of you."

"You will never meet anyone who will love you, so why try?"

"Don't trust him, he's probably searching for a better person."

"She doesn't really love you. Get out before you get hurt."

This mean coach in your head manipulates you and turns you against yourself and the people you love. It encourages hostility, and you soon discover that you are paranoid. You begin to suspect every move your partner makes, and this reduces your self-esteem and drives unhealthy levels of distrust, defensiveness, jealousy, anxiety, and stress.

You soon discover that you are reacting to unnecessary issues and uttering nasty and destructive remarks. You may also become childish or parental towards your partner.

For example, your partner comes home from work and does not have a good appetite, so they politely turn down dinner. Sitting alone after some time, your inner critic goes on a rampage and asks, "How can he refuse my food? What has he eaten all day? Who has been bringing food to him at work? Can I really believe him?" You may begin to act cold or angry, and this can put your partner off, making them frustrated and defensive. They won't know what's been going on in your head, so your behavior will seem like it comes out of nowhere.

In just a few hours, you have successfully shifted the dynamics of your relationship. Instead of savoring the time you are spending together, you may waste an entire day feeling troubled and drawn apart from each other. What you have just done is initiate and enthrone the distance you feared so much. The responsible factor for this turn of events is not the situation itself - it is that critical inner voice that clouded your thoughts, distorted your perceptions, suggested bad opinions to you and, as a result, led you to a disastrous path.

When it comes to the issues you worry about so much in your relationship, what you don't know - and what your inner critic doesn't tell you - is that you are stronger and more resilient than you think. The reality is that you can handle the hurts, rejections, and disappointments that you are so afraid of. We are made in such a way that it is possible to absorb negative situations, heal from them, and deal with them. You are capable of experiencing pain and ultimately healing and coming out stronger. However, the mean coach in your head, that inner critical voice, more often than not puts you under pressure and makes reality look like a tragedy. It creates scenarios in your head that are non-existent and brings out threats that are not tangible. Even when, in reality, there are real issues and unhealthy situations, that inner voice in your head will magnify such situations and tear you apart in ways you do not deserve. It will completely misrepresent the reality of the situation and dampen your own resilience and determination. It will always give you unpleasant opinions and advice.

These critical voices you hear in your head are, however, formed as a result of your own unique experiences and what you've adapted to over time. When you feel anxious or insecure, there is a tendency to become overly attached and desperate in our actions. Possessiveness and control towards your partner set in. On the other hand, you may feel an intrusion in your relationship. You may begin to retreat from your partner and detach from your emotional desires.

There are some critical inner voices that talk about you, your partner, and your relationships. These inner voices are formed out of early attitudes you were exposed to in your family, amongst your friends, or in society at large. Everyone's inner critic is different; however, there are some common critical inner voices.

When you listen to your inner voice, the resultant effect is an anxiety filled relationship, which can mar your love life in many ways. When you give in to this anxiety, you may stop feeling like the strong and independent person you were when you first started the relationship. This can make you thin out and fall apart, which further induces jealousy and insecurity. Attachment and neediness set in, and these put a strain on the relationship.

Chapter 2: Unconscious Behavior Caused by Anxiety

1. Become Clingy

Under certain circumstances, anxiety feelings can make us act desperate and bug our partners. Anxiety can make a person to stop feeling as independent and strong and he/she did before getting into the relationship. Consequently, he/she may find him/herself falling apart easily, acting insecure, becoming jealous, or avoiding those activities that require independence.

2. Control

Our human nature demands that when we feel threatened, we attempt to control or dominate the situation. If we feel threatened in a relationship, chances are, we will try to regain control of the situation. What we fail to realize is that the feelings of threat are not real; rather, they are as a result of the inner critical voice that is distorting reality.

When taking control, we may start setting rules on what a partner should and should not do, who to visit, talk to, interact with, et cetera. This is a desperate attempt to alleviate our feelings of anxiousness and insecurity. This controlling behavior can breed resentment and alienate our partners.

3. Reject

If a relationship is making us to feel worried, a common and unfair defense mechanism is rejection. We start to act aloof, that is, aloof. We become somehow detached and cold. This ensures that if the partner suddenly leaves, we will not feel pain. In other words, new are protecting ourselves by beating our partners to the punch. These actions of rejection can either be subtle or overt. Either way, they are a sure way of creating distance between two partners by stirring up insecurity.

4. Withhold

In some cases, instead of explicitly rejecting our partners because of anxiety, some people tend to withhold from them. For instance, when things have gotten very cross and a person feels very stirred up, he/she retreats. People who use withholding techniques to deal with anxiety in a relationship hold back either a part of their affection of a whole segment of the relationship altogether. Withholding might seem harmless since the partner is not facing rejection of clinginess and control but note; it is one of the gentlest and quietest killers of attraction and passion in a relationship.

5. Retreat

Anxiety leads to fear and being afraid of a relationship you are in can be really stressing. To avoid such stress, a large number of people choose to retreat, that is, giving up on the real acts of love and replacing it with a fantasy bond. By definition, a fantasy bond is a false illusion that replaces the real feelings and acts of love. In this state of fantasy, a person focuses on the form instead of substance. He/she gives up on the real and vital part of the relationship and still stays in it to feel safe. In a fantasy bond, people engage in many destructive behaviors such as withholding or engaging in non-vital activities. The resulting distance leads to the end of a relationship. As much as the retreat will protect you from feelings of fear, it will give you a false sense of safety and you will lose a lot of precious time living in a fantasy. What most people fail to realize is that at the end of the day, they will have to face reality.

Love is a beautiful thing, but truth be told, it has its own demands and consequences. Honestly, love is a very complicated thing.

Over-Analyzing

This is the urge to overthink things, and even literally look for weaknesses or negative aspects. There is a sating that goes, over-analysis causes paralysis. Here is the thing; there is nothing wrong with using logic. In fact, it is okay to be critical or skeptical at least until you figure things out. The ability to think about things thoroughly before accepting them can help you to tell fiction and reality- what is a mere delusion and what is the reality.

However, there is an issue/downside to overanalyzing a relationship. You will never be satisfied with the answer. Everything that is said on done is subject to scrutiny and more cross-examination. A good example of over-analysis and its consequences is when a person n starts to overthink things and consequently creates scenarios in his/her mind, hence basing their actions on imaginary events that have not happened yet.

Picture this; you are on a first or second date. Your clothes, shoes and language give a good first impression. Everything about the prospective relationship looks bright. However, once the partner arrives, you start bombarding them with a bazillion questions about their past relationships. "Have you been in another relationship? How many exes do you have? Why did you leave them? Was there cheating involved? Who initiated the breakup? Are your parents still together? Do they have a good relationship?"

On the brighter side, it is totally fine for a person to express his/her worries about love and being hurt. However, it is absolutely wrong to ask a person some questions that are too personal in the name of protecting yourself. It is wrong on all levels to force someone to recall some things that might be painful for them. Do not ask people questions that make the person feel interrogated. And if you find that you cannot stop yourself from asking these questions, then that might indicate that you are suffering from relationship anxiety. You cannot control your fears about relationships and commitments, therefore, looking for ways to validate your reasons.

Fear of Being in a Serious Relationship

How long can two people take before deciding to be in a serious relationship? There is no specific timeframe. It all depends on the people involved and how well they know each other. Some take three dates, others one month while others might take years before being ready.

If a person has relationship anxiety, his/ her answer to every request for commitment will be "Never" "I am not ready." Regardless of whether the person is in love or not, he/she will not commit to the relationship. The real reason for this lack of commitment is the deep-seated fear at the back of the individual's mind. This person is afraid that he/she is going to end up alone, all over again. Therefore he/she avoids those situations that might set him/her up for betrayal.

Falling in love involves facing real risks. It is about allowing yourself to feel vulnerable. The hard part of love is placing a massive amount of trust in someone else and allowing him/her to mold our hearts. You cannot be 100% certain that the person will actually take care of you. You are not yet sure if the person is the one for you. So, anxiety will make you think "If I am not 100 per cent sure about this person, is there need seriousness?" Then rationalizing a little more, you will get an answer like" If you do not get committed, you will not get hurt" Now, that is an illusion brought to you by anxiety.

In real life, this is what is happening; you are feeling afraid thus reluctant to commit to a person. Consequently, you will never learn through experience. If you are always turning away the chances of love. How will you know the real deal that might help you deal with the relationship anxiety?

You Have a Bad Temper

The most awful thing about relationship anxiety is that it affects the two people in a relationship. In fact, it hurts you and your partner, unfairly. No matter how much the sober person expresses his/her love to the partner suffering from relationship anxiety, this feeling will make him/her look for ways to make the other to feel terrible. For instance, a person can tell you that he/she loves you and relationship anxiety will make you say something like "Do not worry, you will stop." or another bitter thing.

So, what makes you so angry when a person tells you that he/she is in love with you? It is the fact that your brain never allows you to take time off from your dark thoughts. You know very well that these thoughts are irrational but cannot just get past them. They terrorize you every day, no matter what you do. The fear of losing constantly ruins your good moods. Simply, you are mentally exhausted and cannot think rationally. Any minor inconvenience will make you go berserk.

If your partner fails to do things according to plan or says something that does not augur well with what you have determined is appropriate, you start feeling like the relationship is strained. More like someone is pushing the other to make things work. And once you feel bad about the relationship, you start to say painful things or even fight physically. AN understanding partner will forgive you and move on. But remember this; a day will come when that partner gets tired of dealing with your negative energy and raging temper. And when he/she decides to leave, you will develop more relationship anxiety complications.

Too much attachment

Attachment may be positive, but here is the thing, anxiety can make you needy. You will not only be ill-mannered but also, clingy. Why, you might ask, because you are paranoid about the relationship. You are afraid that the slightest silence will evolve into a full-blown painful breakup. That is very unlikely to happen, but, in this irrational state of mind, it seems very much possible.

How can you tell if your attachment is based on relationship anxiety and not real love? First if you are attached simply because you are monitoring your partner, then that is anxiety. If you are oversensitive to cues that might indicate the slightest chances of being abandoned, then you might be having relationship anxiety.

Note, it is very good to remind your partner that you love him/her/your partner to start questioning your real intentions. In fact, it is very sweet to ask for hugs and kisses randomly. But overdoing this can be point-blank annoying.

Being an Extreme Pleaser

Always going that extra mile to impress a partner can be an indicator of relationship anxiety. We have to admit that it feels good to have a partner that arranges for surprises for you. It also feels nice to see the look of happiness and surprise when we do something unexpected for our partners. Giving each other surprises and going the extra mile for each other is very romantic. However, such efforts and sacrifice can be very dangerous if you have relationship anxiety. You might end up doing endless things just to maintain the perfect image for your partner. You might be so afraid that your partner will lose interest in you that you become obsessed with impressing him/her.

You Beat Yourself Too Much

Anxiety causes doubt. You might be the best partner in the best relationship but still, you will feel invalid. You might be doing everything in the relationship but still feel lie it will never be enough. Instead of seeing the good things in front of you, you opt to focus on those things that make you feel bad. You do not have the time to enjoy what you already have.

In the real sense, it could be easier for you to be happier, but your brain tells you that life does not work like that. You believe that happiness is a fake and short-lived experience. The problem is that insecurity will start to push your partner away. Then you will have your fears coming true because he/she will gradually lave.

You Lack Confidence

Sometimes, a person may experience relationship anxiety because of a lack of confidence. Before getting into a relationship, it is important to check on the level of your self-esteem. Having low self-esteem does not mean that you should not get into a relationship, but it is very important to know the status of your heart. Know the state of your mind, heart and soul before getting into a relationship.

Chapter 3: Different Types of Anxiety in Love and How to Overcome Them

Tension prevails in partnerships.

All pairs experience anxiety. Occasionally stress and anxiety originate from troubles at the office or with household and or friends that we carry over into our partnerships. Stress and anxiety can likewise arise from the couple's issues, such as an argument, distinctions in wants or requires, or sensation ignored.

Anxiety Can Negatively Influence Relationships.

Although tension prevails, it can be harmful to relationships. Usually, individuals suppress or keep their anxiety to themselves, which makes it tough for their companions to comprehend what they are undergoing and to supply assistance.

Not managing stress can develop a negative cycle where partners "catch" each other's weight. This happens due to the fact that tension is transmittable-- when our partners are stressed out, we become worried. Think back to a debate that escalated rapidly. You could have "caught" each other's stress and anxiety during the discussion, which made you both feel even more frazzled and made you say things you would not have or else stated. Pairs obtain embedded this unfavorable cycle as well as may be too stressed out to take care of the underlying issue(s).

The Key to Tension Is Just How Couples Handle It.

Couples need to determine as well as speak about what creates their anxiety and what they require when they feel stressed. Although it could be tough to talk about what is producing tension, especially if it is brought on by something within the partnership, it is helpful for companions to speak about their needs and also for partners to supply assistance. Those couples that are most effective in dealing with stress tackle it together. They produce a sensation like they remain in it with each other as well as are a team.

What Can You Do?

Check-in with each other and also pay attention first before you supply options. Ask your partner(s) what you can do to help as well as to make their day smoother. Hug more frequently. It appears weird but embracing for at the very least 30 secs after work each day can assist your bodies to line up and calm each other down. Keep attached throughout tension. Discussing your stress and also having a supportive companion to see you through it makes you as well as your partnership is stronger. Most of us have demanding experiences from time to time because tension can come from numerous sources. Funds. Household stress. Work. Relationships.

And it can have a genuinely distorting effect on our practices. It can make us feel genuinely reduced and also not want to speak to people - with a propensity to close ourselves away and also keep our feelings on the inside.

As well as it can be tough to be self-aware when it pertains to your feedback to tension, very commonly, it can seem like these means of expression are a little outside of your control. Many people find themselves avoiding speaking with others as well as becoming taken out without somewhat knowing they're doing it or unexpected themselves by becoming all of a sudden snappy, cranky and unreasonable.

To offer a little viewpoint on this, our coping mechanisms in these kinds of circumstances are frequently affected by what we experienced maturing. If our parents didn't reveal treatment quickly, we might have become rather experienced at looking after ourselves - indeed, we might have needed to - and so this reaction can kick back in instantly as an adult. Likewise, we commonly duplicate the practices of our moms and dads and also their responses to tension when we're younger.

Just how tension can impact connections

It's not difficult to see why either of these behaviors would affect your relationship adversely. If you're ending up being withdrawn, your partner is most likely to feel pressed away. And also, if you get stylish, they may feel injured or come to be defensive. What can be truly bothersome, though, is that they may intend to help, as well as think that their efforts are being rebuffed. This can feel like an actual rejection, as well as can result in them becoming withdrawn or snappy themselves.

Thus, the problems of stress can snowball as one companion begins to act in an adverse or unconstructive method, so may the various other.

Additional including in this is the truth that they may not become aware of why you're functioning as you are. It might not be quickly evident that it's a tension that's causing you to state unkind points or be unresponsive when talked with. They may feel it's something they have done. This can undoubtedly be mad and also annoying - both for the hurt created and also complication about why it's happening.

Without some type of intervention, the void caused by this kind of circumstance can get bigger and also more significant. And the more you seem like your partner - that, once more, may just wish to assist - gives tension themselves, the much less likely you'll want to try to close that space.

Commonly, the most effective method to proceed in situations such as this is by utilizing a strategy that enables the person experiencing the stress to remain in fee of how much they claim. Very frequently, the very best first step is to say: 'Exactly how can I help simply?' These places firm strongly with experiencing individual problems and are much less likely to make them feel under

And if your companion is open to talking, then the very same emphasis - on them, and their firm - ought to continue to use. Once more, there can be a lure to right away begin to provide remedies or to get them to 'attempt to see the silver lining' - yet, in a feeling, these can be demanding feedbacks in themselves. They can seem like reasoning's, or as if you're disregarding their experience as one that's quickly fixable.

Sometimes, this is precisely the feedback that the cagey person was afraid: one that demands they accede to it, as opposed to one that correctly absorbs precisely how they're feeling, and what they believe.

Instead, it can be a lot more practical to sympathize and also to ask inquiries simply. Very frequently, when we're discovering something challenging, what we want isn't a solution, but just a person to be there with us and provide emotional support. Providing this - even if it implies sitting silently together or simply embracing - might be all they require to begin to seem like the scenario is in control.

Tension can be useful.

Experiencing tension doesn't always indicate your relationship is going to suffer. Instead, your assumption of stress and anxiety-- such as seeing it as a challenge that you can overcome-- is necessary. By watching pressure as a chance to share as well as open with each other, relationships end up being more potent since pairs find out how to browse tension and construct resources to much better deal with future stress and anxiety. Partners discover what they need from each various other and reveal one another that they are looked after, valued, and understood. Having a companion who is there for you as well as reacts to your needs aids your body to manage stress and anxiety better and also makes anxiety feel much less extreme.

Stress

Does that word define your life today? If so, you're not the only one. Most of us experience stress and anxiety. It might be something significant: a new relocation, a health and wellness worry, a harmful partnership. Yet frequently it is something small: a hectic week at work, a youngster house ill on a day loaded with meetings, the post-work/school thrill to put supper on the moment, the last-minute demand from an employer. These tiny everyday inconveniences can add up and also have huge repercussions overtime for our partnerships. Why? Tension in other areas of our life's spills over right into our connections. The work-life problem is a leading source of stress today. Also, research has revealed over and over again that we bring anxiety and even pressure from work and other areas of our lives home with us, hurting our partnerships.

When people are stressed out, they end up being more taken out and also sidetracked, and even less caring. They likewise have much less time for recreation, which leads to the alienation between partners. Stress and anxiety additionally draw out people's worst attributes, which may influence their partners to take out as well, because who wishes to be around someone when they are acting their worst? Gradually, the relationship comes to be more superficial (less we-ness as well as participation in each other's lives), and also couples happen to be a lot more withdrawn, experiencing more problems, distress, and alienation in the partnership.

Stress and anxiety likewise influence our physical as well as psychological health as well as areas extra strain on the relationship. Stress can specifically be bad for couples who remain in rocky relationships since these couples tend to be a lot more strongly affected by daily occasions (good as well as bad) than couples in more steady relationships. However, also for healthy and balanced, stable relationships, tension can create people to see troubles in their relationships that aren't there.

A pair who usually connects well might see their communication break down over an especially challenging week, and also, as a result of the tension as well as sapped sources, they feel like there are real interaction troubles in their relationships. Likewise, a pair which is usually caring may have little love when stressed and also, therefore, pertained to believe that they have an issue with respect as well as time together, instead of identifying it is just the anxiety. These misperceptions can create discontentment with otherwise healthy connections as well as lead people to try to solve the incorrect trouble (interaction, affection) rather than identifying as well as resolving the actual source of the concern (stress).

How to Reduce High Couple Conflicts

The problem belongs to all connections. In an intimate partnership, where the risks are top, as well as sensations, run deep, the problem is unavoidable. Nonetheless, the problem can wear at the fabric of a connection if it is regular or if it crowds out love, love, and also support.

The best study on the dispute in couples was done by John Gottman, the master pairs' study. In one research study, Gottman took an example of high conflict pairs as well as separated them right into two therapy groups. One team discovered problem resolution skills as well as the other group focused on enhancing what he calls the "marital friendship." Pairs in this 2nd group worked on structure trust, goodwill, and also compassion in their relationships. Gottman found that couples who reinforced their relationship reduced the problem to a much better degree than those who discovered dispute resolution skills.

So, what is the message from these two sets of research? If you want to reduce disputes in your partnership, focus on increasing the favorable instead of lowering the negative. Look for opportunities to improve your relationship with your partner. Look for methods to reveal affection and support. Search for chances to produce goodwill and also depend on it. Be kind. Be empathic.

As anybody that has been in a romantic connection understands, differences, as well as battles, are unpreventable. When two individuals spend a great deal of time together, with their lives intertwined, they are bound to disagree every so often. These disagreements can be big or tiny, ranging from what to consume for dinner or stop working on finishing a job to debates about whether the couple needs to move for one companion's profession or choosing youngsters' spiritual training.

Chapter 4: Recognizing Your Anxiety Triggers

Fear of Collapse

This is a sudden fall. It might occur due to peer pressure from close friends who are obvious in one's life, and mostly they always come with shocking words which can cause one to collapse and sometimes eventually die. It can also be caused by a lack of support from one's partner; good support encourages and strengthens love because it is also a bond that fulfills true love. Part of the support includes finance, food, and even closeness to your partner. For the best outcomes, one should avoid peer pressure and negative people.

Just like any other photophobia fears, fear of collapse freezes the heart. Your heart becomes ice-cold, you are constantly thinking that this relationship is going to hit the rock any time, and if you do not do something about it, it will end up destroying your relationship. To recognize this fear, you will see the following.

Suspecting a motive

When your partner tries to show you kindness, for example, take you out for a drink or buys a beautiful dress, all you think of is there must be something he wants, or he has done that is why he is behaving the way he is.

- Trust Issues

You cannot trust anything your partner says, you must go ahead behind his back to find out if he was saying the truth or talking about the exact thing.

- Sticking to the Old Ways

You only want to do things according to the times when you felt like it was working. You do not want to change and experience something new.

- Doubt

You are always in doubt, asking yourself every now and then if it is going to work and still convincing yourself that it might not work.

- Clingy

When you see your partner distancing himself or pulling away, you start being so clingy even after he tells you that he needs some space. It is good to give someone space, this does not mean he is leaving. Being clingy only shows that you have a fear of collapse

Fear of Being Vulnerable

Vulnerability is not always a show of weakness. If you are vulnerable, it only means you trust easily, people can get to you faster; they can understand you better, understand your likes, dislikes, and boundaries and be able to watch their steps when they are with you. It gives you an upper hand, unlike you thinking that it pulls you down. To face your fear of being vulnerable, you will have to point the following signs to know if indeed it is the fear of being vulnerable:

- Not Opening-up

You do not want to open up to your partner because you think he will see you as weak. You prefer to suffer in silence. For example, you have a problem with your parents' home that needs financial help, but you can't tell your partner because you think he will see you as weak. You feel he will think that you are working too, and you must be weak to get help from him.

- Avoiding Conflict

Each time there is a problem in the relationship, like a situation that is more likely to lead to a heated argument or other conflicts, instead of handling it, you let it pass by sugar coating it with fancy dinners, cocktails or even movies so that it won't be a topic of discussion anymore.

- Overprotective

You do not want your partner to understand what is going on in your life clearly. You have put up a shield that should be ventured through. There is a no-go zone in most of your doing even the least important things because you are afraid that if he finds out, he will capitalize on it and you will be seen as weak.

- Overthinking

You are constantly asking yourself a thousand and one questions every time you think of your partner knowing something about you. You are thinking so much about what he will say, how he will react, how he will see you, and so many others.

- Lashing out at Your Partner

This is a defensive mechanism. You do not your partner to go ahead and understand a certain thing about you, so the only way to make him stop and never be interested again is to lash at him. This will keep him at bay from anything that concerns you.

To avoid this in a relationship, partners should be faithful, honest, loving, caring, and stop exposing themselves to that possibility. Lovers should also respect their partner's gargets/devices such as phones for them to acquire peace of mind.

Fear of Not Feeling Important

This is a situation where someone feels not useful to his or her partner. The fear comes in when your lover does not involve you in his or her activities; the partner remaining silent in the house, infrequent communication, frankness, not having sex with your partner whereby sex is the only action that can bond the relationship, Unfaithfulness among the couples. It really hurts due to unexpected changes in the relationship. Some problems might persist; one has to adapt the situation while getting a time of viewing the other partner, in the proses of viewing your partner one should also be patient to give a room for any change.

- Too Sensitive.

You are taking things too personally. Your partner makes a comment, and you think it is aimed at looking down upon you. For example, your partner "honey I think your dress will look better if ironed a little bit". You take this statement super personal, and you start sulking about it because you think that he meant you are useless wearing an un-ironed dress. You start thinking on behalf of him.

- Making a Catastrophe Where It Is Not Needed

You start making a mountain out of an anthill. Your partner calls to say he will be late for dinner and you go to a no speaking spree for a week. Don't you think you are exaggerating things here? He called to inform you early, why are you sulking and not speaking? Because you are suffering from the fear of not being important

- Perfection

Everything you touch or do; you want them to be so perfect in that he will see you as the most important person. You do not want to give him any reason to comment or think otherwise. You are afraid to make a mistake because you think he will see you as useless.

- Panic Attacks

Every time you are looking at your phone to see if he has texted you. If you find that he has not texted, you start panicking. You start feeling less important. You start feeling that you are not among the things he values in his life.

- Doubting Your Every Step

You always doubt what you are doing. You are not sure if it will be good for him so that he can see you as an important person. You are not sure he will like the idea because you want to be the most important thing that has ever happened to him.

Fear of Failure

Fear of failure comes in a person when one does not succeed in his or her plans and oaths of their bond. This makes one be totally discouraged to love another partner; it is caused by things like long sickness, hunger, bad company and idleness, lack of job opportunities. This leads the partner to feel bored, and the true love disappears, the partner seemed to be losing the loved one. To avoid that fear and stress, you should not make it personal, seek advice, share your problem, and let it go.

- Expecting Him to Fix Everything

You are expecting him to be a hero, a Mr. Spider man. You want him to save every situation there is. You want him to walk in your mind and do everything you are thinking of, but if this is not happening, and then you think this relationship is bound to fail.

- Aggressive Response to Passive Questions

The fear of failing is telling you that this must be heard loud and clear and never be repeated again, and you answer aggressively to a simple passive question that he asked. The aggressive response only instills fear in your partner or anger or mixed ideas, and this might ruin your relationship.

- Feeling That the Partner is Un-Reliable

Feeling that you are investing a lot in this relationship than he is, you think he is not reliable; he is not supporting you in anything that matters to you. You feel and think that he is unstable, and he is going to lead this relationship in the wrong path. You think that he is slowly digging the drainage to drain the relationship each time he tells you he is not in a position to attend your exhibition. This is the fear of driving you, and it is important to handle it.

- Having Thoughts That He Will Leave

Each time you are seated, you picture him leaving. You are afraid that he is going to walk out of the door any minute. This all the fear of failures doing, maybe he has no plan of leaving, and it is the fear driving you.

Fear of Entering into Intimacy

If you are asked why you keep on dodging the idea of intimacy you have no answer; this only communicates one thing. You are afraid to get into it. For you to understand that you have this fear, look at how you will know that you have it room in your head.

- Incompatible Schedule

Each time an intimacy topic is brought up and planned when to happen, you say your schedule is not compatible with his.

- Lame Excuses

You are always giving excuses that do not make sense. Like, I just do not feel like it, I do not think it is the appropriate time, and when asked when the appropriate time is or why you do not feel like it, you completely have no answer.

- Am Not Worthy Enough

A feeling of unworthiness has engulfed you. You think he deserves better and that is a more reason as to why not to enter into intimacy. This is all wrong, it is only in your mind and it needs to be corrected.

- Feeling Shameful

Why would you feel shameful to a partner you have been with for a long time? It is not shameful; it is the fear of intimacy.

Past Experiences Ended Badly

Past experiences leave wounds, which causes fear based on their experiences. If you want to realize that you are suffering from this fear, the following are the manifestations:

- Getting Very Angry

A small thing that doesn't need all your anger makes you so worked up because it reminds you of the same thing before.

Always on guard for betrayal signs

You are always waiting for that moment for him to betray you. You are in his phones, diary laptop just looking to find any sign.

- Constantly Thinking That People Will Hurt You and You Need to Protect Yourself.

You are thinking of putting up an out of bounds sign on your face for people to keep off.

- Thinking That Each Time You Get Close to People You End up Being Hurt.

The last time you were hurt because you loved and were so close, this time you are thinking your closeness to another will get you hurt again.

- Thinking That No One Ever Comes to Your Aid When You Need Help. No One Is Ever There for You.

You stood alone in the pain as it tore your heart and you probably are thinking since no one came to your aid, no one is ever going to come and help you when he finally breaks your heart.

Chapter 5: Love Yourself to Love Your Partner

Do You Know Your True Value?

A lot of us look down on ourselves, and we fail to give ourselves the credit that we deserve. We might indeed have gone through experiences that may now affect the way that we look at ourselves. We might have gone through a lot of hurt and abuse and even a very challenging childhood. But these circumstances do not have to continue to define you and hide the unique qualities that make up the real you.

Reasons Why You Are Unique

Just in case you are not convinced about how unique you are, here are some significant reasons proved by science, why you should start seeing yourself differently.

- **Your unique genetic composition is the only one there is and will ever be**: Research has shown that humans are somewhere between 90 -99% different genetically. Such a big difference isn't it? This is to say no one is exactly like you genetically (even if you have an identical twin) and no one can ever be like you completely no matter how hard they try. Why try to compare yourself with or even become someone else when there is only one of you in existence? You simply can't be them, and they can't be you.

- **Your personality is unique**: A person's unique personality is made up of their temperament, thoughts, attitude, behavior, character, and beliefs. No two people will have the same combination of these qualities at every given time. Your personality is how people see you and how they often try to describe you – meticulous, quiet, outgoing, selfless, funny, proud, humble, loud – these are all components of a person's personality, and yours is a unique one.

- **Your experiences are unique**: Your entire life experiences, as well as your day-to-day experiences, are what make you a unique person. There are no two people who have had the same experience throughout their whole lives. Even if you live together, work at the same place, maintain the same schedule, you will find that your point of view of these experiences differs. So, your life experiences are unique to you.

- **Your purpose is unique**: You should believe that you have a unique purpose in this world. You don't have to live the life that someone else has lived. You don't have to be your father or your mother – you should be yourself instead. Even if you follow in their same footsteps you will still find that you cannot produce the same achievements, something will differ from the other, and this difference speaks of the uniqueness of your life and who you are. You have such a unique purpose in life; therefore, you should pursue it and embrace it and not live someone else's life.

Building an Unbeatable Self Confidence That Will Defeat Jealousy Always

The matter of self-confidence is very important when talking about jealousy because a reduced self-confidence can bring about jealous feelings. If you suffer from low confidence, then you are bound to get jealous at some point.

- **Self-confidence can be learned**: Some people have described themselves as not being confident naturally, and they have stuck to that belief from childhood, where it now causes problems with jealousy and the likes in their relationship and life in general. The truth is that even if you are genetically inclined to be withdrawn and shy, that doesn't mean you should have low self-confidence. You can learn to be confident in yourself gradually, and in time you will see the changes confidence can make to your entire life. There are so many people today that were initially not confident in themselves but have grown from that stage into living their dreams and achieving their goals with high confidence. So, if your jealousy is due to an injury to your confidence and is affecting your relationship, believe that you can learn to be confident again no matter your experience or genes and indeed start learning!

- **There are no losers, only winners**: Never see yourself as a failure or a loser at anything you do even if it doesn't work out a hundred times. Life is not a competition, and there are no losers. You are a winner if you choose to see yourself that way and behave like that as well.

- **Life is a process and you can get there as well**: So, you are not where you feel you are supposed to be, so what? And you have tried and failed so many times. We have all failed at something as well, so you are not alone. Some people can't cope with failure and others can't stand the fact that those they consider their mates are getting ahead of them in life, so they turn these feelings to jealousy and anger. You need to understand that life involves process, and the fact that you have failed ten times doesn't mean that you cannot succeed on the eleventh try. Also, the fact that you feel you are behind in life doesn't mean that you cannot reach where you want to be eventually. There are a thousand and one examples of people who have made it great in life but failed initially.

- **There is room for everyone to shine**: Just like the moon and the sun, they shine their light differently, and they don't compete with each other because they know their uniqueness. That is how you should see the world. No one is taking your opportunity or your job. If you didn't get that dream job and someone else got it, you should believe that the job perhaps wasn't for you and you can get another opportunity. Don't imagine the competition and become jealous when someone like that makes a pass at your partner. There is room for everyone to shine our lights as brightly as we desire.

- **Start loving yourself**: It is surprising how some people can love a partner so much and show themselves no love at all. You should start loving the person that you are and treat yourself better. Do things for yourself and be selfish sometimes – it will make you feel great. Treat yourself to something special on occasion. Something that is just for you – a nice spa, an expensive meal, a new dress, anything that screams 'treat!' Start doing things not for others but yourself as well, and you will notice how good it makes you feel. Look at yourself in the mirror when you are all dressed up to go and tell yourself how beautiful / handsome /

gorgeous / sexy / adorable you look. You don't have to wait for someone to say those words to you so you can feel good about yourself. Learn to start loving your unique self and see the boost in confidence that it will bring.

- **Stop doubting your abilities**: The worst thing you can do to your confidence is to question yourself. People will doubt you at least until you can prove them wrong, but when you start doubting your abilities, then there might not be an opportunity to prove anyone right or wrong. Even if no one believes in you, you should still believe in yourself – that is how a lot of people have kept going until they succeeded – by believing in themselves. Whatever it is that you want to embark on, you need to tell yourself that you can. The more you keep feeding your mind with a positive thought, the more your confidence will improve, and you will get better at whatever you try. You can't depend on what people say to give you the confidence that you need, you need to be the first and only coach of your life.

- **Start doing the things that you used to love**: Are there activities you used to love doing but have lost interest in because of how your life has changed? A great way to revive that confidence is to return to some of the things you loved doing like playing a sport or a musical instrument, fishing, skating, singing, dancing, traveling. Whatever it is, start again if it makes you happy – even if you weren't so good at it, this could be an opportunity to get better and do what you love.

- **Try out new interests**: Perhaps you have been passing by a dance school and wondering what it would look like if you enrolled in a class. Or you have recently been interested in playing a musical instrument and have held yourself back because of what your partner or friends might say. You should take that positive step now and try out one or two interests that you have nursed for a long time. It is never too late to try out something new – unless you are physically limited. So how about trying something and if you like it, then continue doing it – you will see that your confidence continues to grow as you make such bold steps.

- **Work on you continuously**: Working on yourself is very important to building a high self-confidence. These are areas that you can start improving. For instance, if you haven't felt confident about your body and have always been threatened when someone with a great body makes a pass at your partner, then why not decide to achieve that great body that you want as well? Remember that you will be doing this for yourself and not for anyone else – it is to make you feel great and confident again. So hit the gym and start working hard to achieve that great body that you want. Perhaps it is something about your appearance or your language that kills your confidence. You can learn how to improve these things as long as it makes you feel more confident. Go get it!

- **Re-assess your company**: One cause of low confidence without even knowing it is the kind of company that you keep. Do your friends look down on you or tell you that you are not good enough for a role or something you want to try? Do you have friends that laugh or mock you when you fail at something? These are confidence killers, and you should avoid them as soon as possible. Great friends should be able to encourage you to reach your dreams and not kill your confidence. So, what kind of things do you hear from your friends? Does it help you grow your confidence? If it doesn't, then you are better off without them. You should stick with friends that are confident and do not see you as a threat to their progress as well. Friends who are secure in themselves and can inspire that in you as well are friends indeed.

- **Take good care of yourself**: Just like I said about loving yourself, you can't love something that you do not care for, so start taking care of yourself. Scientists have shown that taking good care of you can reflect in your overall demeanor and confidence. Pay attention to your hygiene. Take showers regularly, put on clean and appropriate clothing, apply pleasant scents, and pay attention to your hair care. Take care of your living space as well and keep it clean and tidy. Just saying – look great and feel great as well.

When you start to feel so good about your body and environment, it will begin to reflect in your confidence eventually, so try changing up a few things and see the difference it will bring you.

- **Strive to be a better version of you**: Make it a habit of taking regular appraisals of yourself. Where are you now and who do you want to be in one year or five years? Always strive to improve yourself and keep becoming a better version of yourself. Remember that it's not about becoming someone else or competing, but it is all about yourself and building a secure and confident you!

Chapter 6: Ways to Recover Communication with Your Partner

Ask for Clarification

Perception is different from communication. One can pass on a message, but what matters is how it is received. Therefore, clarification is essential, so that information can be received the way it is intended. One way to ask for clarification is to restate what has been said. In case the message was misperceived, the speaker will correct it. It also ensures that one pays attention and encourages the speaker to open up more.

Maintain Neutrality

Emotional intelligence is essential when communicating; one must be informed of their biases and opinions so that the art of active listening can be developed.

When communicating, it is essential to remain grounded. Getting defensive will impede the communication process. As much as people hate critics, one should be open to it, and understand that they are bound to be criticized from time to time.

Listen

Let someone finish their train of thought before butting in and giving one's opinion. Moreover, one should listen entirely and take time to digest the information before evaluating the information provided. It is common for people to get distracted and start thinking of what to respond to before the speaker finishes what they are saying. It is paramount that one has to avoid this type of distraction because it prevents them from genuinely listening to the other person.

Silence

Bouts of silence when communicating allow time for one to digest the information given, it also provides room for evaluation of knowledge and time for a person to identify their biases, and how they might be affecting the listening process. Thus, silence should be used as a tool to sharpen the listening process and promote communication.

During a volatile interaction, silence can be an instrument that is used to bring tensions down. It can also be used to diffuse a conversation that is not productive. It enables parties involved to assess the chat and assess whether it is still within the objectives set.

Use Encouragers

Use prompts to encourage the other person to open up more. The prompts should be minimal so that the listening process is not impeded. Examples include 'oh,' 'uh-uh' and 'then?'

Prompts indicate to the speaker that the listener is following what they are saying and is genuinely interested in what they have to say. Thus, it encourages them to open up more. The listener also pays attention to what is being said because they take an active role in the conversation by encouraging the other person to open up more.

Reflect

Reflection enables the listener to take in the speaker's words. It also helps to connect the body language and other nonverbal cues to verbal communication. Thus, instead of just restating the information, one should take time to reflect the message, and take into account emotions, their background, and why they have the opinion that they have.

Reflection also enables one to make linkages with the information given. At times, one can make a comment, which can be connected to another piece of information.

Reflection is the right way for one to identify their bias, and how it affects the communication process, and decide how to do away with it.

Use 'I' Messages

During active listening, putting feelings into words helps the speaker be objective. When communicating, one might not be aware of the body language they are projecting. This is especially true if they are talking about something sensitive to them. Thus, putting feelings brings objectivity to the conversation.

Validate

Be nonjudgmental to the way the speaker is feeling and validate their emotions. Listen with empathy and understand why they think the way they think. At times, people get extreme emotions from trivial things, and it is okay, as people are entitled to feel, however, they think about issues that affect them.

Validation does not mean that one has to open up about their experiences. The goal is to listen and respond that their feelings are seen, and it is okay to have such feelings. In the communication process, this helps a person open up more.

Redirect

Sensitive topics can lead to aggression, raised voices, or anger. These are emotions like any other, and a person is entitled to them. Thus, instead of making someone feel bad for their feelings, it is better to redirect and talk about something that is not as sensitive.

It can be a brief discussion of a neutral topic, so that the tensions drop, then reverting to the question under discussion after that. If the speaker does not calm down, one can redirect and talk about something else entirely.

Avoid Suing Communication Blockers

Communication blockers make the speaker unable to pass on their points effectively. Thus, they should be avoided at all costs.

'Why' questions make people defensive because they feel like their validity is being questioned. Thus, they should be avoided.

Giving quick reassurances, before a person finishes expressing their point is not advised, because it they will not pass on the information effectively

Another communication blocker is advising the speaker. The goal is to listen and not advise someone unless the speaker asks for advice. Therefore, refrain from giving advice and actively listen.

Digging for information is another communication blocker. People are intelligent and can tell when a person is genuinely listing to them or is digging for information. Once they realize that the listener is doing for information, they clam up and stop communicating. Thus, for effective communication, avoid digging for information, in the pretense of active listening.

Be courteous

Have good manners when communicating. It indicates that the message is essential, and one is more likely to talk more to someone with polite behavior.

Statements like "excuse me', 'pardon me' should be used appropriately, and as stated before, they should be used sensibly to avoid frequent interruptions. They also indicate that someone is following the conversation actively.

Ask Questions

To start a conversation, it is best to start by asking questions. The type of questions that are proposed as a conversation opener has to be neutral. This means that sensitive topics such as religion, politics, and gender have to be steered clear of. Asking questions ensures that a person considers the feelings of the other person first, and quickly learns their opinion on topics that are not as neutral.

Avoid Judgments

Every person on earth has a bias, and this is especially true when it comes to sensitive topics. Thus, to enact emphatic communication, one should avoid judging. One should listen keenly, and refrain from judging the other person at all cost. The other person in the relationship should feel like they are being listened to, and their point of view is being understood. Simply put, when communicating with someone, the listener should be able to walk a mile in the other person's shoes and understand their point of view. In case there are arguments, they should be presented in a manner that is not judgmental.

Pay Attention

There is nothing as unnerving as talking to someone who is not actively paying attention to the communication process. It makes a person lose interest and not open up as much as they want to. Thus, secure communication should be achieved by paying attention to the person speaking, be it in a group or a private setting. Distractions such as noise, phones, and other gadgets should be done away with, and the speaker is given undivided attention. It will enable the listener to identify the feelings of the speaker by reading the body language and respond accordingly.

Refrain from Giving Unsolicited Advice

A popular pitfall to emphatic communication is giving advice or sharing one's point of view, even when the speaker has not sought it. At times, all a person wants is to be listened to. Giving advice that has not been asked for impedes this process, and the person will not be able to communicate their feelings effectively.

Thus, for empathic communication to occur, refrain from giving advice, unless the speaker directly asks for it. Additionally, sharing one's opinion on a subject is good. However, it communicates to the speaker is that the listener is self-centered and does not consider the feelings of other people. At times, giving advice can generate resistance from the other party, and they stop communicating what they wanted to pass on.

Silence

Silence is powerful, especially in a conversation. It makes sure the listener can take in what has been said, and digest it, and give time for summarization. It helps the listener understand what the other person is trying to say and give room for the other person to organize their thoughts.

Short bouts of silence can be used to enact emphatic communication because they are a way for the listener to understand what the speaker is saying. It also gives room to a person to do away with their biases and get the point from the other person's point of view, according to their background. Thus, silence during a conversation should not be seen as awkward, but a practical way to ensure empathic communication.

Managing short instances of silence is a skill that takes time to master. Thus, the listener should practice it so that they do not become awkward or indicate the end of the conversation.

Raise Attention Levels by Self-Detachment and Decreasing Self-Centralization

Seeing a point from someone else's point of view or experience is hard and has to be learned. Thus, to increase attention, one has to detach themselves from their experiences and biases and pay attention to the other person. It helps a person be in the moment, and solely understand what is being said at the moment.

Read the Speaker

People might communicate one thing and mean the other. It happens to the nest of us, especially when we are nervous, or afraid of judgment. However, body language does not lie and will always betray what the speaker wants to say. This is why the listener should read the speaker.

Take Action

Emphatic communication is meeting the needs of the other person. Thus, after being communicated to, one should take action and meet the other person at the point of their needs. It does not have to be the right action, but any activity that would help them overcome their situation.

A person might communicate that they do not seem to get a hold of their finances. An action that can be taken is teaching them simple methods of saving, referring them to someone who can help them. The most important part is their opinion has to be sort on which option is the best and let them make that decision for themselves.

Understand That Perception is everything

Psychology states that empathy involves communication and perception. Communication can occur at any time, but perception is very important, especially when one wants to build an emphatic connection.

People often understand what they want to, depending on their experiences and background. Thus, what is being communicated might not be what will be understood. Stephen Covey once said that "Many do not even listen with the intent to understand; they listen with the intent to reply." Ideally, many people are either speaking or are listening with the intent to reply. Therefore, conversations are like monologues because they are from one person's point of view.

Chapter 7: How to Strengthen the Relationship with Your Partner

1. Start Trusting

L earn to consciously get into the habit of trusting people more. Choose a trusting disposition over a distrustful attitude. Unless you have absolutely concrete evidence about someone, take their word for it. Going around snooping, stalking your partner and behaving like a suspicious maniac only harms your relationship further. Rather, if there really is no reason to be suspicious other than a feeling of insecurity or jealously, let it go.

2. Write Your Deepest Feelings and Thoughts

Journaling is known to be one of the most effective techniques for bringing to the fore your deepest feelings and emotions. It helps you discover multiple layers of your personality to achieve greater self-awareness. It also facilitates the process of an emotional catharsis for venting out pent up feelings. For instance, you may constantly harbor feelings of insecurity because you were raised by neglectful parents or you may never feel you are "good enough" because you were raised by parents who had extremely high and unreasonable expectations from you.

People who have been neglected in their childhood often feel they aren't worthy enough to be loved. This in turn causes them to think that their partner is seeking someone more worthy or deserving of love than them, which creates feelings of insecurity.

3. Regulate Your Negative Feelings and Emotions with Mindfulness

Mindfulness is a great way to calm your nerves and manage runaway emotions. Tune into your physical and mental self by identifying your feelings, thoughts and emotions by taking deep breaths. Try and detach yourself from overpowering negative emotions such as jealousy and insecurity. Every time you find yourself overcome with thoughts of jealousy or insecurity, practice mindful meditation.

4. Be Frank and Accepting About Your Feelings

Discussing your insecurities with your partner will help you create a frank and open communication channel. Rather than doing and saying crazy things to your partner, be upfront and share your feelings. Say something similar to "I apologize for bothering you regarding your friendship with ABC, but it is not my lack of trust in you. I simply feel insecure about it."

5. Avoid Suffocating Your Partner

Start relaxing a bit by letting go of your desire to imprison your partner. The harder you try to imprison someone against his/her own will, the more forcefully they'll try to escape your domineering behavior. Let your partner have the freedom to spend time with his/her friends, talk to their attractive colleague or do other things that otherwise make you feel threatened. Once they realize how secure and confident you are about the relationship, they will automatically be drawn to you. A secure and self-assured partner can be extremely irresistible.

6. Create Boundaries as a Couple

Sometimes people behave in a certain way without even being aware that their actions negatively impact loved ones. You may find your partner indulging in flirtatious behavior often, but he/she may believe it to be a part of their fun personality. They may not even be aware of the damage being caused to you or the relationship. For them it may be a harmless display of their charm and wit.

Setting boundaries early in the relationship will keep you both on the same page as to what is appropriate or acceptable behavior and where to draw the line. You both can mutually discuss and arrive at the "non-negotiables" in your relationship. Is harmless flirting alright with both of you? What about kissing on the cheek? Dancing with a member of the opposite sex? Once clear boundaries are established, your partner will be less likely to behave in a way that can upset your or incite feelings of insecurity. Talk issues through, look for a common ground and once everything is clear – learn to trust your partner unless there is compelling evidence to believe otherwise.

7. Go to the Bottom of Your Insecurity and Negative Emotions

It can be really hard to objective assess why you feel pangs of insecurity each time someone compliments your partner, or he/she speaks warmly with his/her colleagues. It can be highly tempting to blame another person for your emotions. However, getting to the root of your insecurity by being more self-aware is the foundation to free yourself from its shackles. Take a more compassionate and objective look at the origination of your insecurity. Think about the potential causes for feelings of insecure.

For instance, if you find yourself being increasingly insecure of your partner, know why you feel it. Is it because you don't want to lose him/herDo you suffer from a false sense of self-entitlement that your partner's time belongs only to you? Do you feel what you feel because of a sense of inadequacy that constantly makes you think "you aren't good enough?" Once you identify the underlying reasons causing feelings of jealousy and insecurity, it becomes easier to deal with your behavior.

8. Switch Off from Envious and Insecure Mental Chatter

Tell yourself to mentally shut up when you find yourself engaging in self-defeating jealous self-speak. You can use several techniques to achieve this. It can be using a stop or "x" sign whenever negative thoughts begin to pick momentum in your mind. Condition yourself to stop unexpected thoughts with practice sessions using visual and mental reinforcements. Try saying stop really aloud when you find yourself embarking on a destructive insecurity self-talk journey. This way you will embarrass yourself more and realize how ridiculously you are behaving. The idea is to train your brain into thinking that it isn't alright to come up with insecure self-talk.

9. Avoid Judging Other People Based on Your Past

Ever notice how suspicious people are always suspicious of others? Or liars think everyone around them is lying? Our perception of people and their motives is often a reflection of who we are. Stop using your past or present behavior as a yardstick for perceiving your partner's actions. For instance, if you have a history of being involved with married men/women, do not assume that no married man/woman can ever be trusted and start mistrusting your spouse. Just because you did or are doing something does not mean he/she is indulging in it too.

10. Discard past Relationship Baggage

A strong reason why you are always paranoid about your current partner cheating on you can be traced back to an earlier relationship. You may have had an ex-partner horribly cheat on you with your best friend. The betrayal may have had such a severe impact that you view every relationship in a similar distrustful light.

Painting everyone with the same brush can be a disastrous mistake in any relationship. There is a solid reason your earlier relationship did not last, and you should leave the garbage of your earlier relationship where it belongs – in the trash can.

11. Question Yourself Every Time

Each time you find yourself feeling even remotely jealous; question the underlying feeling behind the complex emotion of jealousy. Is the insecurity a consequence of my anger, anxiety or fear? What is it about this situation that makes me jealous? When you question your jealously critically, you are a few steps away from taking constructive steps to convert a cloud of negativity into a bundle of positivity.

12. Insecurity Is Not Always an Evil Monster

It may sound contradictory to everything we've been discussing about insecurity, but truth is insecurity may not always be harmful. Sometimes, a tiny amount of it may actually do your relationship a whole lot of good. How? It can sometimes motivate you or your partner to safeguard your relationship. If expressed in a productive and wholesome manner, insecurity gives you the much-needed impetus to protect your territory. Insecurity helps you assume the role of a protector for your loved one and/or relationship, and this can be good if it doesn't scale extreme heights. Be smart enough to realize when jealousy goes from being a relationship protector to a relationship destroyer. You choose whether it is a boon or bane for your relationship.

13. Remind Yourself of Your Strengths Periodically

Each of us possesses unique strengths that set us apart from others. Keep reinforcing to yourself how wonderful you are through positive affirmations and visualizations. You will find yourself feeling less insecure when you are aware of your positives. The more self-assured and confident you are, the less affected you will be by other people's actions. Know where your strengths lie, keep doing things that make you feel great about yourself and believe that you are worthy of true love.

14. Focus on Productive and Positive Ideas

Rather than obsessing over who your partner is cheating you with, try to develop interests outside of your relationship. Do not make it the nucleus of your existence even if it means a lot to you.

15. Imaginary Fears Do Not Necessarily Mean It Will Actually Happen

We need to understand that our insecure hunches do not necessarily mean the act is actually occurring. Just because we fear something is going to happen doesn't mean it will happen. A majority of the times our fears are totally unfounded, and not even remotely close to coming true. Just because your partner is somewhere else, and you fear he/she is with someone else doesn't really mean he/she is actually proposing relationship on a date. Understand the difference between thoughts and actual events. The make-believe imaginations of our destructive mind are often far from reality.

16. Be Generous

Spend more time giving and helping others. This will not just make you feel great about yourself but also help you develop a greater understanding of how you add value to others' lives and how they would be grateful to have what you have. Volunteer within your local community by helping folks read and write English or preparing meals for the less fortunate or even assisting a friend who is struggling to finish college.

17. Stay Away from Insecurity Triggering Situations

Be aware of situations that trigger elements of jealousy and insecurity in your behavior and avoid these situations whenever you can. For instance, if you are a person who can't help experiencing pangs of insecurity each time your partner mingles with members of the opposite sex, avoid dating a person who generally hangs out with the opposite sex and is extremely popular with them. This will invariably lead to friction unless you work a common ground.

18. Focus on the Positives

So, you witnessed your partner flirting with one of his friends. Big deal? Not really. Keep in mind that you both have a history of intimacy and an incomparable closeness, which is why you are together in the first place. There's a unique spark about your togetherness that cannot be matched by others. Just because someone pays their friends a few compliments and displays warmth doesn't necessarily mean they want to be with him/her for life. Sometimes, people just flirt to lighten the mood or break the ice or make the other person feel good about himself/herself.

Remember the really positive and unusual things about your relationship every time you are overcome with feelings of insecurity/jealousy. Remind yourself of your wonderful moments, of everything your partner has told you about why he/she fell in love with you, and the loving things you have done for each other.

19. Do Not Be a Party to Relationship Games

People often try to feel great about them by purportedly getting their partner to feel insecure. Do not fall into the trap. Displaying any signs of insecurity will only encourage your partner's behavior. Tell your partner firmly that indulging in a jealousy/insecurity inducing behavior only demeans him/her and won't make him/her feel any better about him/her. Even if you feel jealous, try to keep a stoic and unaffected demeanor, which should eventually stop these excruciatingly uncomfortable, attention-drawing tactics.

Chapter 8: How to Help Your Partner to Overcome Anxiety

Loving a Person with Anxiety

This part is dedicated to partners of people who struggle with anxiety. Relationship and love demand that we get involved in our partner's life and this means we always have to be supportive and loving. If you have a partner with one or more types of anxiety, you are already aware of how it can influence not just the relationship, but your life too. Anxiety comes in many forms, and there is no magic pill that can help. Anxiety is also an individual experience that can differ in many ways. The list of things we can do to help our partner when they are having an anxiety attack differs from person to person.

Acute Anxiety

Acute anxiety happens out of the blue. It can be caused by different things, certain situations or other people you and your partner meet. It happens suddenly, and there is no time for planning and taking it slow. You need to be able to react in the moment and to know how to assess the situation. Understand what is happening, what your partner is going through, and come up with the right way that can help neutralize the anxiety. There are four steps you can take to be supportive and helpful in case of acute anxiety:

1. Be calm, be compassionate. If you are not, you won't be able to support your partner needs at that moment. If you give in to anger, frustration, or your own anxiety, it won't help. It can even make things worse. You also need to remember not to give in to your partner's anxiety and accommodate it. In the long run, this is not helpful. Instead, offer understanding, not just solutions.

2. Assess your partner's anxiety. What level is it? What are the symptoms and signs of an anxiety attack? An anxiety attack can hit with a different strength each time. You need to be able to recognize it to choose actions appropriate to the given situation.

3. Remind your partner of the techniques that helped with anxiety attacks. Whether it is breathing or exercise, your partner is probably aware of their success in neutralizing anxiety. But in the given situation, maybe he or she needs reminding. Once they are on the right path of dealing with anxiety, your job is to provide positive reinforcement. Give praise and be empathetic once your partner executes techniques that will help with an anxiety attack.

4. Evaluate the situation. Is your partner's anxiety attack passing? If it is, be supportive and encourage your partner to continue whatever he is doing to lower his anxiety. If it stays at the same level, or increases, you should start the

steps from the beginning and come up with different techniques and strategies to help your partner with an acute anxiety attack.

Chronic Anxiety

To address chronic anxiety, you might have to try out exposure therapy, as it is considered the golden standard of treatment by many people. Usually, it takes the guidance of a professional therapist to try with exposure therapy. But, if the level of your partner's anxiety is not severe, you might feel comfortable enough to try it on your own. In this case, you have to act as a guide and learn how to be a supportive person for your partner.

You have to start with the least challenging situation and progress slowly and steadily towards more challenging ones. If anxiety isn't decreasing in the first challenge, it's not time to go to second.

For example, let's say your partner has a fear of heights. He or she wants to overcome this fear and be able to climb the buildings last floor. How will exposure therapy look in this case?

1. Tell your partner to look out the window from the ground floor for exactly one minute.
2. Climb to the second floor together with your partner. Remember that you are not just an exposure therapy guide; you also need to act as a support. Make them look out the window from the second floor for one minute. In case of

anxiety showing up in its first symptoms, remind your partner to do breathing exercises to lower its impact.

3. Once your partner feels better, they should try looking out the window again.

4. If no anxiety presents itself, you should leave your partner's side. They need to be able to look through the same window, but this time without you.

5. Climb to the third floor and repeat steps three and four. When your partner feels ready, continue to the fourth floor, sixth and so on. If your partner's anxiety is too high, don't hesitate to stop. The first session doesn't need to take longer than 30 minutes.

6. Each new session needs to begin with the last comfortable floor your partner experienced. You don't need to always start from the ground floor, as your partner progresses, feeling no anxiety when looking through the window of the second, third, even fourth floor.

7. Take time. Your partner will not be free of the fear in just a few days. Be patient and continue practicing exposure therapy in this way until your partner can achieve the goal and climb the last floor.

8. The goal of exposure therapy is not just to get rid of fear and anxiety. It should also teach your partner that he or she can control and tolerate discomfort. Your partner will have an opportunity to practice anxiety-reduction techniques in a

safe and controlled environment, with you in the support role.

Specific Disorder Interventions

Under the guidance of a trained therapist, the two of you will learn how to approach it in the best possible way. Your partner's therapist might ask you to join in a few sessions, and he will teach you how to better help your partner in situations that elevate anxiety. If your partner is not diagnosed, but both of you suspect he might have a certain disorder, advise your partner to visit a doctor. Self-diagnosing can lead to mistakes, and you will make wrong choices in how to approach your partner's anxiety.

Panic Disorder with Agoraphobia

If this is your partner's diagnosis, you two probably already have a pattern of behavior that is designed to accommodate your partner's anxiety. You probably follow your partner to social events, and you are the one who is in charge of running errands outside of the house. This accommodation is counterproductive in the long run. You are showing that you care, love, and support your partner, but it prevents him or her from experiencing a full life. Your partner needs to learn how to overcome anxiety. You may approach panic disorder with exposure therapy, so your partner becomes less dependent on you:

1. Choose an errand that your partner thinks he can handle himself. It can be shopping, going to a doctor appointment alone, walking a dog, etc.

2. Plan what errands are more challenging for your partner and add them to the list. Write them down as "to be accomplished in the future." It is important to work slowly but keep a clear vision of what needs to be accomplished.

3. Work together on slowly accomplishing the first task on your list. If it's going shopping alone, accompany your partner a few times, so they are accustomed to the environment. When he or she feels confident enough to go alone, let them. Encourage and support their decision.

4. Once your partner accomplishes the task, be there to discuss his experience about it. Listen carefully and address any issues that might arise. Encourage your partner and keep track of his progress.

Obsessive-Compulsive Disorder

When it comes to OCD, what you can do for your partner is not to engage in his behaviors. Also, encourage him not to give in and repeat their compulsive behaviors. If you give in and comply with your partner's OCD, you will not be helping. Although it will surely elevate the tension made by your partner's OCD, complying will reinforce the fears. For example, if your partner asks you to go to the kitchen and make sure all appliances are off, you shouldn't comply. But you should also not argue or call your partner irrational. It is ineffective, and it will only deepen the anxiety.

Discuss with your partner how is it best to approach anxiety and agree on a strategy. This is where a professional therapist will be of most use to both of you. A professional can guide you through this conversation and help both of you feel comfortable discussing the delicate topic of your partner's disorder.

You will need to learn how to change from saying things like:

"I will not go to the kitchen again, you are imagining things, and being irrational" to "I appreciate your concern about the kitchen appliances, but we agreed that the best thing we can do is to help you learn how to manage the feelings you are having right now."

Your partner will agree for their own benefit that the best thing you could do is stay by their side, not check the kitchen, and help them work through the anxiety. This can be done with breathing exercises that will help your partner calm down. In time, your partner will show less fear. The OCD will decrease, and you will feel less frustrated.

Generalized Anxiety Disorder

The behavior of people with GAD is similar to that of people who have OCD. They have fears about certain things, and these fears are not comforted by reassurance. GAD usually creates concerns that we all have. It can be about finances, health, and school. But people with GAD will overblow the proportion of these fears, and they will influence their daily life. If your partner is diagnosed with GAD, you are aware of how simple problems we face every day can sound like total catastrophes. Your partner probably assumes the worst possible end of certain situations.

It often happens that people with this affliction develop a constant feeling of inadequacy. They believe they are not good enough for their partners, and that they never will be. When this happens, they usually try to overcompensate and make everything perfect so their partner can love them. On the other hand, some may feel that there is nothing they can do and that there is no point in trying. They underperform reinforcing their feelings of inadequacy.

Social Phobia

Social phobia comes in many forms. It can make going to work a very difficult task, or it can make maintaining relationships impossible to achieve. A therapist uses the technique of testing the hypothesis of a patient. This is a very successful way of bringing realization to the patient that their fears and anxieties do not have a foundation. A therapist can teach a person with social phobia the basic communication skills to prepare them for situations they might encounter in their endeavors to overcome anxiety.

Post-Traumatic Stress Disorder

PTSD is caused by experiencing a traumatic event, and it can affect every aspect of a relationship. If your partner is suffering from PTSD, he or she will react to certain triggers that will remind him of the traumatic experience. In the case of PTSD, anxiety attacks can happen both spontaneously and routinely. Often people who have PTSD become disconnected from their partners when anxiety hits them, they become unresponsive to their partners, or they don't even recognize them for what they are.

Make a Plan for Relieving your Partner's Anxiety

Now you know potential techniques you can use to reduce your partner's anxiety. Use this knowledge to create a plan, make a list of practical actions and ineffective actions for when your partner experiences anxiety attack. It is important to remember what to do in situations that trigger anxiety, but it is also important to know what not to do.

Chapter 9: Exercises and Remedies to Overcome Anxiety

A Healthy Relationship Is a Good Relationship

A healthy relationship makes both partners feel safe. Only when there is a basis for protection will individuals and the couple grow and mature. Intimacy is possible only if people feel safe enough to be vulnerable. Any conflict without it threatens the whole relationship.

It is possible that some of the people I see in counseling will end their marriages. Some certainly should never have happened at all. These are the couples who were unable to establish and maintain their partnership with others. Some of them married for all the wrong reasons: to get out of a parent's house for money, or just because everyone else expected them. Many combat verbal, physical, or emotional violence. In-such situations, it is vital to ensure the protection of individuals first. Only then should a couple think about trying again.

Nonetheless, most of the couples I saw in practice do not battle the repercussions of marriage without love or violence. They have come for advice because they long for the link they once had, or they don't function. "We can't communicate" means "we're not communicating," and it often does not feel sufficiently comfortable for one or both of them to be 100% connected.

Loving alone isn't adequate. Security depends on attitudes and behaviors, which foster emotional connection and deep mutual respect. If one felt insecure, distrustful, or challenged emotionally, marriage would obviously not work in the long-term. It may last — for many reasons, people remain in unsatisfactory relationships. But it's not going to be personal.

A marriage-should be a safe place for every partner to be loved, respected, and seen and to have a strong sense of cohesion. A good marriage is one where each partner regularly works on the following security elements:

· **Security**

Safety depends on ensuring that the other person is committed to the promise of commitment and does everything he can to fulfill this promise. Every wedding has rough patches. Each marriage has periods when the partners feel out of sync. Commitment to commitment ensures that the issues are dealt with by both parties. They're not disengaging or bailing. We don't allow themselves to lay blame. Each of them has a duty and works hard to fix their role in that gap between them.

· **Trust**

Confidence is a gift that we give to someone we love. It's a fact in a healthy marriage. Everybody knows that the other person would never do anything to break their hearts. You treat it as a precious commodity because you realize that once destroyed, it is challenging to recover trust, couples who are last couples who do not betray the faith. Since trust is so vital for security and because circumstances can be misread, either I leap to conclusions about treason. Instead, they speak through one of the partners when they feel betrayed.

· **Honesty**

All partners must be frank with each other in order to trust. Since neither of them has anything to hide, phone and computer passwords are exchanged. Their investments, actions, and relationships are real. You understand that a couple is a team of two, and each of them needs the integrity of the other to function.

· **Mutual respect**

In healthy marriages, the partners appreciate and love the other person, and often say so. We respect the opinions, goals, thoughts, and feelings of each other.

· **Fidelity**

Fidelity means various things to various people. It is not beneficial to say that when you think about it, you both, of course, have the same thing in mind. A happy couple has spoken openly and honestly about how they interpret "cheating" and their expectations of each other. You make a mutual agreement that you intend to uphold.

- ### Platinum Rule

It is a good rule, but the Platinum rule takes things a step further: "Treat someone as they want to be handled." It means taking the time to consider and to do what most respects and pleases your partner even if you don't want that to be.

- ### Emotional accessibility

The partners are emotionally involved in successful marriages. All frequently show love. They both share their thoughts and emotions and are open to their mate. If a conflict occurs, no one shuts down mentally. Alternatively, they meet and support each other while working through anything that is disturbing.

- ### Clean fighting

Sure. Yes. Sometimes everyone loses it. But one can be upset without the other individual being weakened. Calling, bullying, intimidating, threatening to leave, or throw out the other person are aspects of dirty struggles. Those who deal with a dispute by physical or emotional violence never settle it. Usually, the situation is much worse than it had to be.

Sanitary couples know how to fight with dignity. I don't blame them. Instead, they speak from their own feelings and experiences.

Last marriages are founded on health. Without the relationship, no member of the couple will relax. Every person thereby becomes a better version of themselves, and marriage becomes stronger and more intimate.

You must be both interested in good contact in your partnership. This needs you to be genuinely interested in what your partner says and responds in kind. You should also show your feelings plainly, for a stronger relationship. This lets him know exactly what's happening to you, which fosters a deeper connection and a better relationship. Nevertheless, this relationship is not a static object. It moves through its ups and downs through the different stages. What are these stages? Let's take a look. Let's take a look.

The Six Stages of a Relationship

According to life and organizational strategist Tony Robbins, the six (6) phases of a partnership are clearly defined.

1. Love and Passion

This is the step when your partner is the only thing on your mind. The chemistry between you is correct, and you are invested in your partner's success. All your acts are designed to lose yourself and help you achieve them.

2. Not Enough Romance

You both love one another, but you sense a void deep within. You wish your partner could fill this, but you can't.

3. The relationship of convenience

The romantic dimension has dissipated in the third stage as the relationship progresses. This is not so much devotion, not so much passion. You cannot, however, separate yourself because you have other ties to keep you from doing so. You're living with the family (when you have children) or because it's too difficult to get rid of mutual financial obligations and responsibilities. "You may live together with your partner, and you may be happy, but there's no profound emotional involvement. Whether you focus on work, hobbies, family (other than your partner), friends, etc., most of you are probably in Position Three. What is challenging is to believe your partner is a right person— not lovely enough to get excited, not bad enough to quit.

4. Planning your escape

In stage 4, the relationship brings you no pleasure. In reality, you still think of how wonderful life would be if you weren't with your current partner.

5. Don't want to be in a relationship

In the fifth stage, you want to communicate with someone.

6. You're not in a relationship, and you don't want to be in one

You've given up relationships now. You don't want to let anyone come close to you. You've had a bad experience, and you don't want to ruin it. Which level do you feel at the moment? Write it down. Write it down. Sensitivity is the first step towards any positive change.

The Six Human Needs in Relationship/Marriage

Here is a breakdown of the six human needs:

1. **Certainty:** You must make sure in your relationship you are relaxed, i.e., you have enjoyment free of pain. However, for some people, particularly those who long for spontaneity, it can be monotonous and boring, to make sure that everything is perfect.

2. **Variety:** It is the need for variance and variety ety "spice things up" and keep things more exciting in the relationship. You want variety and tasks that exercise your emotional and physical scope.

3. **Significance:** It feels good to know that you are important, special, necessary, and desired.

4. **Love / Connection:** This is the need or need for a deep connection with another human being and a sense of true belonging.

5. **Growth:** "If we stop growing, we die," it was said. It is important in every facet of life-spiritual, emotional, and intellectual-to continue to grow.

6. **Contribution:** This is the ability to go beyond one's own needs. As Tony Robbins says, "All things in the world benefit or are destroyed outside itself." Whether it's time, money, energy (or all three), it's all worth it and makes you feel like a whole person. Which of these six human needs are your first and second motivations? What's your partner like? Problems arise when in our relationship, we do not meet the primary and secondary needs of each other. Now that you know the phases and human needs in a relationship, I hope you have found out where the partnerships and interests (as well as your partners) fit into the scheme. Let us take a look at the things that one or both of you most likely do.

Why Couples Argue

There are lots of reasons why couples fight and argue about differences in-laws, quality time spent together, or jealousy. Let's look at those. Let's look at those.

1. **Sex:** There is typically a disconnection at some stage in this type of intimacy. Perhaps your partner is not as open as you

are in your bedroom or vice versa. You may not also be happy that you feel you deserve.

2. **Money:** Couples fight for money, too. Your costumes might not represent your partner's. Such discrepancy also leads to tremendous disagreements, which can even end the relationship.

3. **Kids:** Children are another major topic that creates a divide between couples. The preference of parenting style, in particular. You may be strict in your parentage, but your partner is more relaxed. If children gravitate to the lenient parent, the harder parent may feel tired of being the "bad guy." This could then lead to discord and a sense of being left out or unbearable. Even before the rugrats are born, fights will begin. You might, for example, like your grandma to name your child, but your partner may prefer to use "northwest" as a certain celebrity couple did. You may have differing opinions, even though you are not parents, on whether or not you both want children, what religious or cultural system they are taught, or how you want them to be educated. All these communications must be answered as soon as possible.

How Communication Works in Relationship

Many in troubled relationships say,' We don't talk anymore.' They probably mean that they don't communicate any more effectively. The truth is that people still connect. Sometimes two people who treat each other quietly interact with each other.

The five traditional forms of marriage communication:

1. Emotion
2. Touch
3. Spoken or written communication
4. Context of the situation
5. Non-verbal physical expression (facial expressions, expressions, gestures, behavior, etc.)

It is easy to concentrate only on words, but only a fraction of the information pairs share.

Conclusion

Anxiousness does not have to derail your life or the life of your partner. If you are in a relationship where anxiety is an issue, you should take comfort in knowing that anxious symptoms can be managed effectively in various ways, relieving the hold that anxious thoughts have on your relationship. Part of what makes anxiousness so difficult to manage in relationships is that many people do not have an accurate understanding of what anxiety is rendering the simple act of recognizing it a difficult one.

Anxiety can be defined as an emotion characterized by excessive worries or fears. It is this anxious emotion that allows a class of disorders referred to as anxiety disorders to be described.

Perhaps the most well-known anxiety disorder is what psychologists refer to as generalized anxiety disorder. This is the disorder that some people are referring to when they talk about anxiety, although it is estimated to account for slightly less than fifty percent of all cases of anxiousness. A common category of disorders characterized by anxiety is the specific phobias. Specific phobias are associated with excessive fear around a specific object or trigger, like crowds, spiders, or speaking publicly.

The first step to successfully dealing with anxiousness in the relationship setting is to educate yourself enough on the subject so that you can understand the condition and all the ways that it may surface in a relationship. The goal of the first was to give you a thorough understanding of what anxiety is and why anxiety may be more common in certain parts of the world and certain groups. This allows you not only to approach the anxiety in your relationship from the standpoint of knowledge, but it also permits you to show sympathy for your partner's anxiety because you understand it better and have an idea of where it may be coming from.

Being fully educated about worry requires that you have a basic understanding of anxiety disorders. Although many relationships may be characterized by the general anxiety that is associated with generalized anxiety disorder, other conditions like panic disorder, specific phobias, obsessive-compulsive disorder, or post-traumatic stress disorder have unique symptoms which makes dealing with them a unique ordeal. The goal is not necessarily that the reader should know how each disorder should be managed, but at least to be able to recognize what type of anxiety their partner suffers from and to be aware that different types of anxiousness should be managed differently.

The question of where anxiety comes from is a loaded one. Although it has been observed that this condition does frequently run in families, it has also been found that anxiety appears to be more common in Western countries than developing countries (in addition to other notable demographic trends). A potentially important cause of anxiety is the dysfunctional relationships that some men and women may experience in their youth. This is the idea behind attachment theory: the model that shows how children learn how to interact with other people and their environment based on the relationship they have with their primary caregiver.

Anxiety can be treated successfully, providing relief for the millions of men and women in relationships and out of them that deal with anxiousness. Anxious symptoms can be treated with medication, but it can also be treated successfully with therapy, dietary changes, and natural remedies. These natural remedies include things like herbs found in the environment, inositol, and transcendental meditation. Although more research has to be done to show how effective these treatments are, they represent another option for people looking for alternatives to the more common medication and therapeutic options.

This would not be an effective about dealing with anxiousness in relationships if it did not provide the reader with tips, they can follow to help them maintain their relationship in the face of worry. It is not easy dealing with anxiousness either as the individual suffering from it or as the partner of the anxious individual, and this is a concept that this recognizes.

An important fact to know about anxiety is that it usually does not go away on its own. If anxiety is left untreated, it will persist, potentially derailing the anxious individual's familial and romantic relationships and preventing them from forming new, enduring ones.

Love is enjoyable when you let go of the anxiety that comes between you and your partner. When you give anxiety a chance to run free in your love life, it may be difficult to know when and how to react to some sensitive situations. This may lead you to feel indifferent or unconcerned to some vital relationship issues or put on a show of being uninvolved and forceful when speaking with your partner. While it's certainly not your fault, it's beneficial to understand how anxiety may be affecting the manner in which you see things.

When it feels like anxiety is genuinely keeping you down, you will need to overcome it both for your well-being and for the health of your relationship.

Anxiety is love's most noteworthy executioner. It makes others feel as if you are suffocating them. It's not easy to overcome this, but it's possible.

Anxiety makes it hard to realize what's important and what's not. It can blow things out of proportion, distract us, and cripple us. But it doesn't have to control us.

You deserve to be in a happy, loving relationship that isn't marred by anxiety's vicious grip. All it takes is conscious effort and a new perspective to realize that anxiety's weakness is a loving connection. By strengthening your relationship, you weaken anxiety's grasp. What's a better example of a win-win than that?

CPSIA information can be obtained
at www.ICGtesting.com
Printed in the USA
BVHW060744220321
603170BV00005B/898

9 781801 741682